The Culture of Us

Franklin Pacheco

illustrated by:
Hatice Bayramoglu

Hey son how was your First day of **school?**

Today I had fun my teacher is nice, and it's a big class

We spent the whole day playing games and getting to know each other

Well that sounds terrific, are you excited for the **school year?**

You bet; but I have a few questions

O really – sit down and let's talk about it

What's on your mind son?

Wasn't today a fun day?
Today was fun a lot of kids looked like
me but spoke funny and had
strange last names,

some did not even speak English

Mom tells me I am black, are they black
like me?

O 'I see, well the short answer is yes

You see, I had the same question when I was **young**

I spoke to your granddad about it

He took me to the park, to show me a

few things and **tomorrow**

I will do the same; as for now let's get some **rest**

A Kite!

Are we going to go fly one?

You bet your button dollar

we are going to have so much fun

just you wait and see

Okay, let's go!

Today I am going to give you a world view

You see this kite is **magical**

and we are going to fly to a few

different countries; all we need is a good

gust of wind,okay?

so hold on-- up, up and **away!!!**

The Bahamas

Clara

Ocean
Atlantique

Pinar del Rio

Matanzas

CUBA

Cienfuegos

Victoria de
Las Tunas

Camagüey

Holguin

Manzanillo

de Cuba

Welcome to **Cuba**

Cuba is a Spanish speaking country that

is very **diverse**

here they have a lot of immigrants from

Jamaica and Haiti that have

migrated

and settled within the eastern part of
the island

You see son the **Caribbean Sea**
touches a lot of other countries

thus creating **trade** and
opportunities

for those who seek it

Cuba is one of many islands

we are going to visit

are you ready?

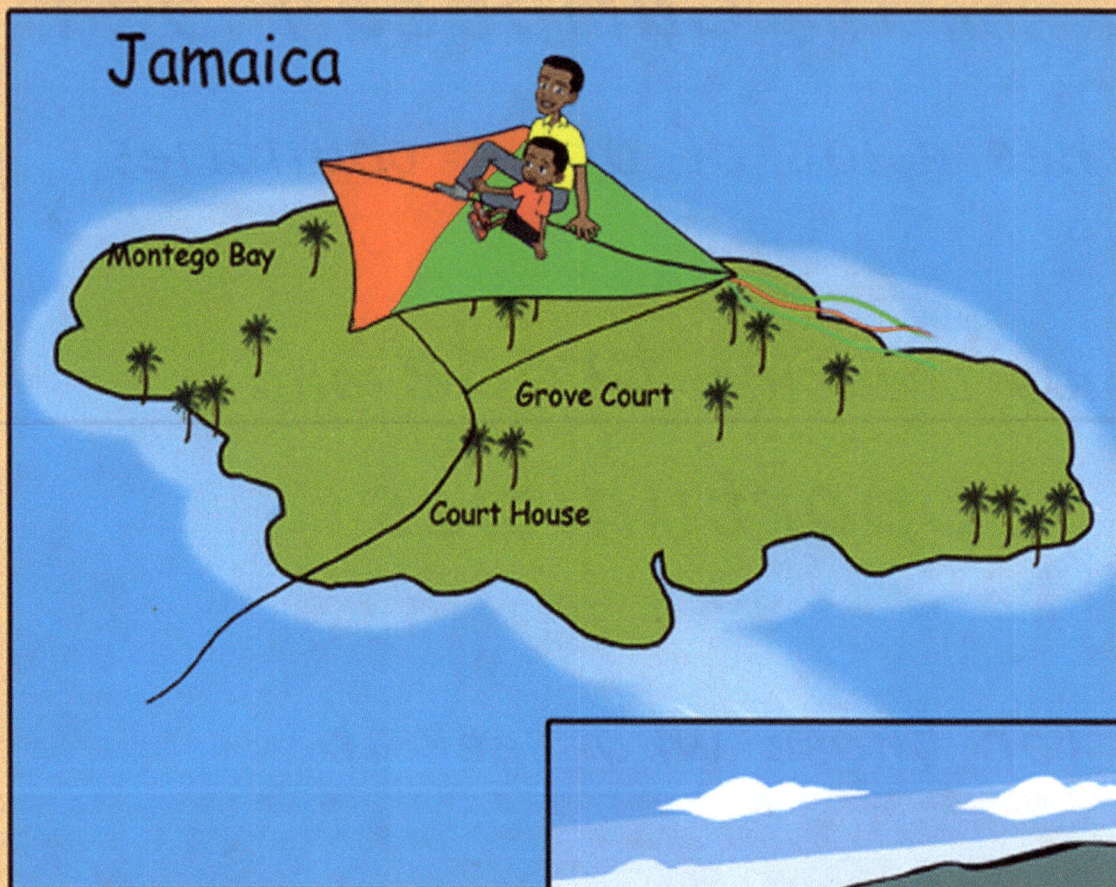

Welcome to **Jamaica!**

Here the British took control instead

of the **Spanish**

which resulted in a language called

Patois...

An english dialect spoken in the British

carribean by people of African descent

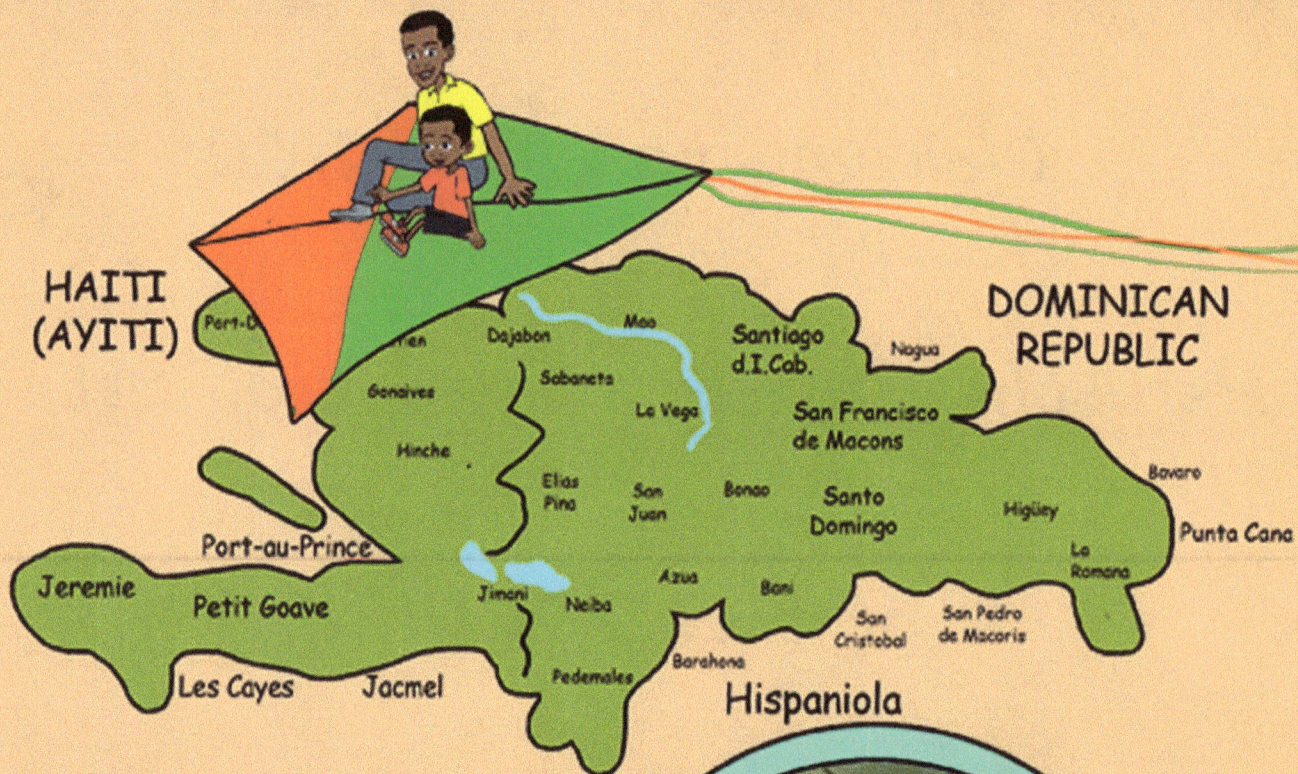

HAITI
(AYITI)

DOMINICAN
REPUBLIC

Port-D...

...ien   Dajabon   Mao   Santiago   Nagua
                              d.I.Cab.

Gonaives   Sabaneta   San Francisco
                 La Vega   de Macons

Hinche   Bavaro

         Elias   San   Bonao   Santo   Higüey
         Pina   Juan   Domingo   Punta Cana
                                                    La
Jeremie   Azua   Romana
         Port-au-Prince   Jimani   Bani
      Petit Goave   Neiba   San   San Pedro
                                          Cristobal de Macoris
   Les Cayes   Jacmel   Pedernales   Barahona

                              Hispaniola

Our next stop is the island of
Hispaniola,

the island is comprised of two countries
Dominican Republic a Spanish
speaking country and Haiti a French
speaking country

Haiti was the first country in the
Caribbean

to be independent from colonial rule
Creole, which means a mixture of two
languages is widely spoken here

As we go through

Dominican Republic

you can see why

they are known to have the largest
lakes

and tallest mountains

in all the Caribbean
The favorite sports pass time here is
Baseball

Costa Rica! home of the amazon rain forest,

this country has a British Caribbean side, just like Nicaragua

Around 1850, many Jamaicans arrived to Costa Rica looking for opportunities

The province of Limon is a result of the migration

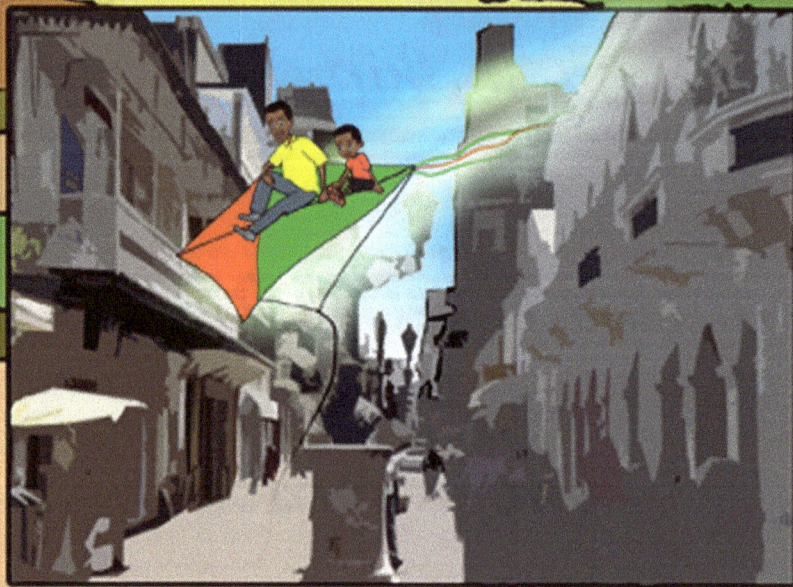

Nicaragua!!!

Most importantly **Bluefield's,**
Nicaragua

a chief Caribbean port in which hardwood, shrimp and lobsters are exported

Africans first arrived here when a Portuguese slave ship crashed on the **Miskito cay**
slaves from Jamaica seeking freedom arrive during the 19th century

Bluefield's is known for carnival

Every neighborhood is represented
during carnival and at the end they dance

to celebrate fertility,

the **culture** is infused with Spanish
which has resulted in a language called

Creole
The creole here is a mixture of
Spanish and **English**

Brazil, the largest country in South and Latin America.

Dad from what I can see there are a lot of kids that look like me in every country we visited

Bingo! That is correct, remember it is not uncommon to be black and **mix** at the same time, due to our world history Brazil was colonized by the Portuguese and a big part of the population is mixed like the others we visited

I had **fun** today dad,

can we go out next week to see more

countries?

Certainly, maybe we will bring Mom

along for the ride

Hey,

you two were have you **been?**

I have been **worried** sick

Hey mom,

dad took me to the **park,** and we had
grandpa's **Kite**

We started flying ......

Say, no more, your Father always raves

about **Grandpa** and his kite!

www.ingramcontent.com/pod-product-compliance
Lightning Source LLC
Chambersburg PA
CBHW061955090426
42811CB00006B/941

9 781646 061228